MW00831591

Front Cover Photo Credit. The cover design contains a rock from the top of *Gordon's Calvary* obtained when my husband, our son Steve, and I climbed that hill in 1968. The crown of thorns was purchased in the Old City of Jerusalem, and the three rusty nails were obtained from the ruins of a fire on the Temple Mount by our Arab guide, Elijah. It also pictures an ancient New Testament Improved Version upon the basis of Archbishop Newcome's New Translation with a Corrected Text and Notes Critical and Explanatory. From the London edition, Boston. Printed by Thomas B. Wait and Company, Court Street I 1809, for W. Wells. This ancient New Testament was a gift from Wiley and Pat Patterson.

I would like to thank Byron Tyler, lifetime friend of my family, for his excellent photography and the gracious gift of his time.

Therefore!

I Hope in Him

Joyce Rogers

Published by
Innovo Publishing, LLC
www.innovopublishing.com
1-888-546-2111

Providing Full-Service Publishing Services for
Christian Authors, Artists & Organizations: Hardbacks, Paperbacks,
eBooks, Audiobooks, Music & Film

THEREFORE! I HOPE IN HIM

Library of Congress Control Number: 2015947438
ISBN 13: 978-1-61314-292-9

Cover Design & Interior Layout: Innovo Publishing, LLC

Printed in the United States of America
U.S. Printing History
First Edition: August 2015

Dedication

I dedicate this book to my five very special children,
their families,
and my beloved husband.

Stephen Michael Rogers

Gifted musician and writer. Called of God to place his daddy's Pastor Training Institute and The Adrian Rogers Sermon Library into the lives of the following generation of pastors. Married to Cindi (Bradley). They have one daughter, Adrienne Renae Hetzer (married to Brian Hetzer), and one grandson, Townes.

Gayle Christine (Rogers) Foster

Gifted speaker and entrepreneur (in top leadership of Premier Design Jewelry), married to Mike Foster. They have two musically gifted sons, Michael (classical guitar) and Adrian (organ).

David Curtis Rogers

Compassionate church planter in Spain for eighteen years. Gifted writer and chief editor of The Adrian Rogers Sermon Library. Married to Kelly (Mason). They have two gifted, grown sons, Jonathan and Stephen. Awarded a Doctor of Theology degree by Southeastern Baptist Theological Seminary in 2015.

Janice Lynn (Rogers) Edmiston

Homemaker, gifted speaker, Sunday school teacher, independent representative of Premier Design Jewelry. Married to Bryan Edmiston. They have three daughters, Angie Luce, married to Nathan; Rachel Kendall, married to Eric; and Breanna Edmiston; and one son, Andrew Edmiston. She is a grandmother of seven—Marianna, Adrienne, Graham, Poppy Joy (who lives in heaven), Luce, Allie, and Pierce Kendall.

Baby Philip Gentry Rogers

Born on his brother Steve's fourth birthday, caught up into the arms of Jesus through sudden crib death at two and a half months old on Mothers' Day. Because of him I learned the greatest lesson of my life—how to totally depend on Jesus.

And to their devoted father
and my beloved husband
of fifty-four years,
Adrian Pierce Rogers,
man of courage, conviction, and compassion.

Special Tribute
to my godly sister

Doris Swaringen

In His presence
July 2015

Wonderful friend and prayer partner

"I'll miss you greatly!"

Appreciation

I want to express my deepest appreciation to the following people:

Bart Dahmer, president of Innovo Publishing, for seeing worth in publishing my book, *Therefore! I Hope in Him.*

Darya Crockett, my gifted editor who helped me in so many ways to improve my manuscript.

Steve Rogers, my oldest son who read my manuscript and gave invaluable suggestions and encouragement.

Nancy Bramlett, Lee Ann Spradlin, and Rhonda Sinquefield, special friends who read my manuscript and wrote recommendations.

Audrey Davis, for proofreading my book.

Contents

*"Hebron therefore became the inheritance of Caleb
. . . because he wholly followed the LORD God of
Israel" (Joshua 14:14).*

*". . . therefore, our God, we thank You and praise
Your glorious name" (1 Chronicles 29:13).*

*"You have delivered me . . . Therefore I will give
thanks to You, LORD . . . and sing praises to
Your name" (Psalm 18:48–49).*

*"Therefore we will not fear, even though the earth
be removed, and though the mountains be carried
into the midst of the sea . . ." (Psalm 46:2).*

sorrow and mourning shall flee away" (Isaiah 51:11, KJV).

"Therefore will I divide Him a portion with the great . . . because he poured out his soul unto death" (Isaiah 53:12).

"Therefore . . . we look for light, but there is darkness!" (Isaiah 59:9, KJV).

". . . therefore . . . this thing has come upon you" (Jeremiah 40:3b).

"Therefore I hope in Him!" (Lamentations 3:24b).

"Therefore do not worry, saying, 'What shall we eat' or 'What shall we drink?' or 'What shall we wear?' . . . But seek first the kingdom of God and His righteousness . . ." (Matthew 6:31, 33a).

*"Therefore whoever confesses Me before men, him
I will also confess before My Father who is in
heaven" (Matthew 10:32).*

*"Therefore I say to you, do not worry about your
life . . ." (Luke 12:22).*

*"Therefore, having been justified by faith, we have
peace with God through our Lord Jesus Christ"
(Romans 5:1).*

*"Therefore we were buried with Him through
baptism into death, that just as Christ was
raised from the dead by the glory of the Father,
even so we also should walk in newness of life"
(Romans 6:4).*

*"I beseech you therefore . . . that you present your
bodies a living sacrifice . . ." (Romans 12:1).*

Preface

The title of this book is *THEREFORE! I Hope in Him.* It has been said that, "When you see the word *therefore,* you ought to see what it's there for." I have a penchant for doing word studies in my quiet time with the Lord. Sometimes a word captures my attention, and I draw a circle around it.

One such word is *therefore.* In every instance, there is a truth that precedes this word. I am always eager to discover what that truth is and how it can apply to my life. God has laid on my heart personal experiences and applications for twenty-nine of these occurrences. They have greatly blessed my life, and it is my prayer that they will be a blessing to yours.

The conclusion is *THEREFORE! I Hope in Him.* Jesus is the One in Whom all my desires are fulfilled.

Chapter 1

"Hebron *therefore* became the inheritance of Caleb . . .
because he wholly followed the LORD God of Israel"
(Joshua 14:14).

———————————

Adrian and I stood in the Valley of Eschol in Hebron, Israel, surrounded by acres of beautiful vineyards. We were reminded that God gave Hebron to Caleb because he followed the Lord God of Israel with his whole heart.

When the twelve men were sent to spy out the land, only two, Caleb and Joshua, came back with a *good* report. They said, "You should see the fruit! It takes two men to carry one cluster of grapes." They said, "Yes, there are giants in the land, but our God is able to cast them out." The other ten spies brought back a *bad* report and said, "Yes, it's true about the luscious fruit, but there are giants in the land, and we are like grasshoppers in their sight. We are not able!" (See Numbers 13:30–33).

Many years later, God honored the faith of Joshua and Caleb. To Joshua He gave the leadership of this new nation. To Caleb He granted his desire and gave him the Valley of Eschol, where enormous grapes grew.

Today, Hebron is still a fertile land that produces delicious grapes in abundance. If we, like Caleb, follow the Lord wholeheartedly, surely He will give us a *land* where the fruit of the Spirit grows love, joy, peace, longsuffering, kindness, goodness, faithfulness, gentleness, and self-control (Galatians 5:22–23).

We will have to fight for this land—to conquer the giants of hate, fear, doubt, impatience, and the like. But as we put our faith in our great God, He will conquer these giants, fighting through us. Then we will possess the *promised land* of Spirit-filled living.

Chapter 2

". . . *therefore*, our God, we thank You and praise Your glorious name" (1 Chronicles 29:13).

I taught a new church members' class for children for over forty years. One of my lessons was on the five kinds of prayer: *confession, praise, thanksgiving, intercession, and petition.* I told the children that I thought that *praise* and *thanksgiving* were the Siamese twins of prayer. As physical Siamese twins are joined somewhere, so God's spiritual Siamese twins—*praise* and *thanksgiving*—are "joined at the hip," so to speak. They are different but always joined together.

Yes, *praise* and *thanksgiving* are different. *Praise* is telling God that we love Him and telling Him how wonderful He is. *Thanksgiving* is saying thank You to God for all He has done for us. Every day I get up praising God for Who He is and how much I love Him. Then I reflect on what He has done for me. My husband, Adrian, *graduated to glory* just a week before Thanksgiving Day. It had always been my habit on that day to make a list of all the things I was thankful for that year. I thought, *Why should today be any different?* I still have that list that begins with my gratitude for Jesus, my Lord and Savior, followed by many blessings about Adrian and our wonderful family, for which I was grateful. Then came the blessings God had given to us at the four churches we had served through the years. God has been so faithful to me! How could I do anything else but praise and thank Him?

I love to sing my praises to God. Almost every day I get up singing to Jesus how much I love Him. I am so thankful for His presence in my life. Oh, I miss Adrian! I think about him every day. However, I am not lonely because I have claimed Jesus to be my spiritual Husband. He has promised to never leave me!

Chapter 3

"You have delivered me . . . *Therefore* I will give thanks
to You, O LORD . . .
and sing praises to Your name" (Psalm 18:48–49).

———————————

Psalm 18 is my favorite chapter in the Bible. It is all about deliverance—God's deliverance of David when he was hiding from King Saul. David called God his rock, his fortress, and his deliverer (v. 2). He was surrounded by his enemies—the sorrows of death, the sorrows of hell, and the snares of death (vv. 4–5).

In his distress, David cried out to his God. Verse 6 says that God heard his voice. We suppose that there will be immediate deliverance, but not so! No, then there was an earthquake and after that the darkness set in (vv.7–9). Have you ever been there? Has there been an earthquake in your life—an unexpected illness, a divorce, even death—and it got oh so dark? I've been there in the darkness! But it was then that God showed up. God makes darkness His secret place (v. 11).

Yes, God came down and darkness was *under* His feet (v. 9). I've also been there when God showed up. It was so dark that first night when I went to bed alone after Adrian made his journey to heaven. I cried out to God, "Help me! Help me!" And do you know what? He did! God was there in my darkness and shone His light on me. As He did for David, so He did for me—"He sent from above, He took me; He drew me out of many waters" (Psalm 18:16).

Then, oh then, deliverance finally came. "He brought me forth also into a large place; he delivered me, because he delighted in me" (Psalm 18:19, KJV). The one who was "the delight of my earthly life" had taken his flight to his heavenly home. But "the delight of my soul" promised to never leave me.

One of my favorite promises in God's Word is Psalm 18:29 (KJV): "For by thee have I run through a troop; and by my God have I leaped over a wall." I can see Him in my spiritual mind's eye. He grasped me by the hand and with His strength *we* ran through a troop of troubles. Then watch me leap over that wall—that wall of fear, of worry, of loneliness, and of sorrow, holding on to His hand.

We are on the other side. Praise God, *we* have won the battle! He gave great deliverance to David and then to me. Yes, He will also give great deliverance to you.

Chapter 4

"*Therefore* we will not fear, even though the earth be
removed, and though the mountains
be carried into the midst of the sea . . ." (Psalm 46:2).

Which one of us who was alive on 9/11 doesn't remember where we were when the Twin Towers came crashing down? Our granddaughter Renae called on the phone long distance and simply said, "Turn on your TV." We asked, "Which channel?" She replied, "Any channel." So Adrian and I ran to the television and were aghast as we saw one, then both, of the World Trade Center towers crumble. Then the Pentagon was hit, and a plane crashed in a field in Pennsylvania.

It was a horrible day! Almost instinctively my husband called for a prayer meeting at our church. At 11:00 a.m., people started streaming into the seven-thousand-seat auditorium. It was packed! The people were afraid. We all began to cry out to God!

The Lord directed my thoughts to Psalm 46. This is what verse 2 says: "Therefore will not we fear, even though the earth be removed, and though the mountains be carried into the midst of the sea." But before the *therefore* came this assurance in verse 1: "God is our refuge and strength, a very present help in trouble." I later discovered that the president's wife, Laura Bush, had also found solace in this comforting passage from God's Word.

Without God, we have plenty to make us afraid, then and now. Then, we did not know who the enemy was. We later found out that the instigator to this horrid plot was Osama bin Laden. Now he is dead! But Al-Qaeda is still very much alive and ISIS, extreme Islamic terrorists, has vowed to either convert everyone or destroy them. Many have been beheaded for the name of Christ rather than deny His holy name! These terrorists are greatly deceived and believe that their God, whom they call Allah, wants them to conquer all nations in his name and to kill all Christians, Jews, and anyone who doesn't agree with them. But our God is Jehovah! He is the God of Abraham, Isaac, and Jacob. He is above all other gods.

Chaos exists all over the world. Indeed, there are "wars and rumors of wars," as the Bible has predicted (Matthew 24:6; Mark 14:7). Is it the beginning of the end times? As Adrian used to say, "It is getting gloriously dark!" I could be tempted to be afraid. My "earthly protector" is no longer here. But this one thing I know: **God is in control!** He has promised to never leave me nor forsake me (Hebrews 13:5b). He is the One Who makes wars cease.

When chaos surrounds us, what are we to do? Panic? No! The answer is found in verse 10: "Be still, and know that I am God; I will be exalted among the nations, I will be exalted in the earth!" A comforting truth is given in Psalm 46:7 and then repeated in verse 11. "The LORD of hosts is with us; the God of Jacob is our refuge. Selah."

I can go to sleep tonight trusting in our great God.

Chapter 5

"... *Therefore* in the shadow of Your wings
I will rejoice" (Psalm 63:7).

Pat and Charles Mason, my son David's in-laws, had a home for many years that they named Shadow Wings. It was a place of physical refreshment for them, their family, and friends. I have been there and experienced the blessing of this place of refuge. Adrian died a week before Thanksgiving. I found love and rest at Shadow Wings during those days.

The scriptures tell me that in the shadow of His wings I should rejoice. The reason *why* I should rejoice is given at the beginning of this verse: "Because You have been my help ..." God has helped me in so many ways:

> He gave me His presence in my loneliness.
> He gave me peace in my storm.
> He gave me protection from harm.
> He gave me provision for my every need.

I have also made a study of promises about the covering of His wings. This verse indicates that I will find shelter in the shadow of His wings. I can also find *spiritual* refreshment here.

Sometimes we don't feel like rejoicing, but we can rejoice *by faith.* Remember, He is your help. Indeed, He will help you! Then one day you will be surprised by joy, and you will even *feel* like praising our great God.

I remember what Adrian once said, "You don't know how much you need Jesus until Jesus is all you have." Yes, my earthly protector and provider is gone, but I still have Jesus. I have claimed Him as my spiritual Husband. Indeed, He is enough!

Chapter 6

"Therefore with joy you will draw water from
the wells of salvation" (Isaiah 12:3).

Many years ago, Adrian and I visited Jacob's Well in
Nablus, Samaria. At the well, the guide drew water
in a bucket and each person in our group took a drink. I
sang the song, "Fill My Cup, Lord!" and Adrian shared
the story of the Samaritan woman at the well.

This woman came to draw water from the well.
Jesus met her there and challenged her to ask for a drink
of *living* water. He told her of her sinful lifestyle and
showed her the great need she had for salvation. She had
lived a very immoral and unhappy life, always looking for
joy in a new relationship. She finally found a satisfying
relationship in that Man Who offered her a drink from
the well that never would run dry.

A modern woman was looking for happiness.
She had not found it in religion, so she tried looking
in a bottle. Of course, that drink did not satisfy. She

27

finally found a relationship with a Man named Jesus. He satisfied her thirst. He gave her living water from the well that shall never run dry. I know that woman. Jesus gave me a great love for her. I have been so blessed to witness her changed life.

I knew another thirsty woman. Her heart was bowed with grief. She came to her Savior and asked for His relief. Then Jesus took her burden and left her with a song. And now she is rejoicing in Jesus all day long. I know because I was that thirsty woman.

> Fill my cup, Lord
> I lift it up, Lord;
> Come and quench
> this thirsting of my soul.[1]

---

[1] Hymn, "Fill My Cup, Lord," lyrics and music by Richard Blanchard.

Chapter 7

"*Therefore* thus says the Lord God: 'Behold, I lay in Zion
a stone for a sure foundation, a tried stone,
a precious cornerstone, a sure foundation . . .'"
(Isaiah 28:16).

———————————

Jesus told a parable. He said that a wise man built his house upon a rock. However, a foolish man built his house upon the sand. When they were young, I taught my children to sing these words, "The rains came down and the floods came up, but the house on the rock stood firm."

My husband always used this parable when he performed a wedding ceremony. He encouraged each couple to build their home on Jesus—the Rock of Ages, the firm Foundation, the precious Cornerstone. Numerous hymns of the past, and songs of the present, have been written about this Rock. "Rock of Ages, Cleft for Me," "How Firm a Foundation," and "Cornerstone" are just a few.

The land of Israel is a land filled with rocks. When Adrian and I traveled there, I was reminded about the many songs written about Jesus, our Rock of Ages. I sang them as we traveled along. It was my great privilege to climb the hill of Calvary on several occasions with Adrian and our two sons, Steve and David.

A Muslim cemetery has occupied the top of Calvary for two decades. It is covered with tombstones and giant thorns. The first time Adrian, Steve, and I climbed this hill was in 1968. I picked up a rock, some smaller stones, and some thorns for souvenirs. I have the rock displayed with a picture of Adrian and Steve climbing that hill.

The Muslims discovered that Christians were climbing the hill and put a stop to it. You must now stand either at the foot of Calvary or from a vantage spot in The Garden Tomb to look at the top of this rugged hill. I do not put my faith in places or spots, but they remind me that this is still a place of death and a curse. It is Jesus' death for me somewhere on that hill that counts for all eternity. Praise God, He took my curse upon Himself. He also died for you and has taken your curse. Now we are free!

Chapter 8

"Therefore the LORD will wait, that He may be gracious
to you . . ."* (Isaiah 30:18).

———————————————

No one likes to wait. At the doctor's office, they even have a waiting room. Sometimes after we wait we receive bad news. Other times we receive good news. Isaiah tells us that God is a God Who sometimes waits. His purpose in waiting is that He may be gracious, that He may have mercy on us. In Psalm 59, verses 10 and 17, He is called "My God of mercy." In verse 10, the psalmist says, "My God of mercy shall come to meet me." "The multitude of His tender mercies" is spoken of six times in the scriptures.

> Psalm 5:7 "But as for me, I will come
> into Your house in the multitude of
> Your mercy."

Psalm 51:1 "Have mercy upon me, O God, According to Your lovingkindness; According to the multitude of Your tender mercies . . ."

Psalm 69:13 ". . . O God, in the multitude of Your mercy, Hear me in the truth of Your salvation."

Psalm 69:16 "Hear me, O LORD, for Your lovingkindess is good; Turn to me according to the multitude of Your tender mercies."

Psalm 106:7 "Our fathers in Egypt did not understand Your wonders; They did not remember the multitude of Your mercies . . ."

Lamentations 3:32 "Though He causes grief, Yet He will show compassion According to the multitude of His mercies."

He has an abundance of mercy. The 23rd Psalm is probably one of the most loved passages in the Bible. It concludes with this thought: "Surely goodness and mercy shall follow me all the days of my life . . ." (Psalm 23:6a). Goodness and mercy are my constant companions. Yes, sometimes God wants to show mercy. Then we are told that we will be blessed if we wait for Him. No, we don't like to wait, but I can testify to the fact that we will be blessed when we learn to wait in His *waiting room*. He is molding us to be more like Him. He also is making us strong, so we can endure the trials that come our way.

"But those who wait on the LORD shall renew their strength. They shall mount up with wings like eagles, they shall run and not be weary, they shall walk and not faint" (Isaiah 40:31).

Teach me, Lord, to wait—patiently!

Chapter 9

"'*Therefore* you are My witnesses,' says the LORD,
'that I am God'" (Isaiah 43:12b).

———————————

Isaiah the prophet repeats over and over these words from God: "I am the LORD; I am God; I am He." In Isaiah 44:6 he said, "Thus says the LORD, the King of Israel, and his redeemer, the LORD of hosts: 'I am the First and I am the Last; besides Me there is no God.'"

The false cult of Mormonism teaches that before Jehovah existed there was another God and that we can become gods. What blasphemy! There is but one God—His name is JEHOVAH.

I sing in my church's choir. I love the song we sing that expresses this thought: "There is no God like JEHOVAH." Indeed, there is none. He is beyond compare.

He is omnipresent—everywhere
He is omniscient—all knowing

He is omnipotent—all powerful
He is the one and only God!

Chapter 10

"*Therefore* the redeemed of the LORD shall return, and come with singing unto Zion; and everlasting joy shall be upon their head: . . . and sorrow and mourning shall flee away" (Isaiah 51:11, KJV).

J ust think of this magnificent promise for everlasting joy—that sorrow and mourning shall flee away! I believe it! I have been to Jerusalem, yes, to Mount Zion, and have sung His praises there. But there is coming a day when all of us who are redeemed shall come to Zion with singing. There will be no more sorrow and tears.

I have personally known sorrow and crying. From time to time when memories flood my soul, tears will come, but one day they will be wiped away forever. I fasten my thoughts even now on the joy of His presence. I am not lonely because I have claimed His promise that He will never leave me.

Yes, it is the redeemed who will come with singing and joy. I am one of the redeemed. Are you? You can be by trusting in that precious blood that He shed for you on Calvary and by trusting in His resurrection from the dead.

> Redeemed, how I love to proclaim it!
> Redeemed by the blood of the Lamb;
> Redeemed through His infinite mercy,
> His child, and forever, I am.
>
> Redeemed, redeemed,
> Redeemed by the blood of the Lamb;
> Redeemed, redeemed,
> His child, and forever, I am.[2]

---

[2] Hymn, "Redeemed—How I Love to Proclaim It," lyrics by Fanny Jane Crosby. Public domain.

Chapter 11

"*Therefore* will I divide Him a portion with the great . . .
because He poured out His soul unto death"
(Isaiah 53:12).

One of the greatest chapters in the Bible is Isaiah
53. In the last verse of this great Old Testament
passage is a *therefore*. *What* has gone before? *Who* was this
chapter all about? *Who* poured out His soul unto death?
I know what I think, but let us examine these words of
the prophet Isaiah. In fact, let's go back a little into Isaiah
52 and look at the description of the *Who*.

> 52:14 "So *His* visage was marred more
> than any man, and His form more than
> the sons of men."

> 52:15 "So shall *He* sprinkle many
> nations."

53:2a ". . . *He* shall grow up before Him as a tender plant, and as a root out of dry ground." (See also Luke 2:52.)

53:2b "*He* has no form or comeliness; and when we see *Him*, there is no beauty that we should desire *Him*."

53:3 "*He* is despised and rejected by men, a Man of sorrows and acquainted with grief."

53:4 "*He* has borne our griefs and carried our sorrows." (See also Mark 15:15.)

53:5 "*He* was wounded for our transgressions, (See also Luke 22:23.) *He* was bruised for our iniquities; The chastisement of our peace was upon *Him*, And by *His* stripes we are healed." (See also Mark 14:65; 15:15, 17.)

53:6 "The LORD has laid on *Him* the iniquity of us all."

53:7 "*He* was oppressed.
He was afflicted
He opened not *His* mouth." (See also
Matthew 27:12.)

53:8 "*He* was taken from prison and
judgment . . ." (See also Matthew 27:1–2.)
"*He* was cut off out of the land of the
living;" (See also Matthew 27:50.)
"For the transgressions of My people
He was stricken." (See also Matthew
8:17.)

53:9a "*He* made *His* grave with the
wicked—but with the rich in *His* death .
. ." (See also Matthew 27:57, 60.)

53:9b "*H*e had done no violence, nor
was any deceit in *His* mouth." (See also
Matthew 27:23.)

53:10 "It pleased the LORD to bruise
Him; He has put *Him* to grief. ["My
God, my God, why have you forsaken
me?" (Matthew 27:46)] When You
make *His* soul an offering for sin, (see
John 19:30) *He* shall see *His* seed, (see

Romans 8:16) *He* shall prolong *His* days." (see Matthew 28:6)

53:11 "*He* shall see of the travail of *His* soul, and shall be satisfied. "*He* shall bear their iniquities." (See also Matthew 8:17.)

It is obvious that this is a *man* to whom Isaiah 53 refers.

He was despised.
He was afflicted.
He was wounded.
He was oppressed.
He was taken from prison.
He bore their iniquities.
He was cut off.
He made *His* grave
    with the wicked and
    with the rich in *His* death.
He had done no violence.
He has put *Him* to grief.
He shall prolong *His* days.

Who is this man? To me it is so clear. This man is Jesus! The New Testament affirms this in Matthew 8:17: "That it might be fulfilled which was spoken by Isaiah the prophet, saying: 'He Himself took our infirmities and bore our sicknesses.'" Multitudes of people agree that this is a prophecy about Jesus. Yes, He was despised, afflicted, wounded, and cut off. He was raised from the dead, fulfilling the prophecy in v.10b that "He shall prolong His days." But others do not see this. Many Jews believe that it refers to the Jewish nation, but the nation is not a "He." A nation cannot bear the sins of the people.

Yes, there are other references in Isaiah to Israel, the servant of the Lord. But this chapter refers to One Who was of the lineage of David of the nation of Israel. That One is Jesus, Who was called the Son of David, the One Who suffered, bled, and died for all the world. But He was raised from the dead and lives for all eternity. He was the *suffering Servant*, Who paid for *my* sins, was *my* substitute. Yes, He can be your Savior if you will only believe and receive Him.

Chapter 12

"*Therefore* . . . we look for light, but there is darkness!"
(Isaiah 59:9, KJV).

There was a time in ancient Israel similar to today (Isaiah 59:14). Take a look at the constant unrest in the Middle East. It doesn't take much surmising to conclude that we, indeed, *walk in darkness*. Everyone is looking for light at the end of the tunnel. As I am writing today, I'm sitting in the Atlanta airport waiting for my flight to Florida. There is a TV monitor in view, and it is playing an up-to-date report of the Israeli-Gaza terrorist war.

For several weeks, rockets have been fired from the Gaza Strip into Israel. Israel has a protective dome called the Iron Dome that has resisted the rockets. The latest and most severe threat is the tunnel system from Gaza into Israel. Even today, Gaza militants have failed to infiltrate Israel. There have been at least thirty-four tunnels presently discovered and destroyed by the Israeli military.

The Bible tells us that in the end times the whole world will stand against Israel. No one would have ever thought that the United States would turn against Israel. Is that day approaching? I hope not, but we will have to wait and see.

The Light of the World Is Jesus

The whole world was lost
In the darkness of sin;
The light of the world is Jesus.
Like sunshine at noonday
His glory shone in;
The light of the world is Jesus.

Come to the light
'Tis shining for thee;
Sweetly the light
Has shined upon thee.
Once I was blind,
But now I can see,
The light of the world is Jesus.[3]

---

[3] Hymn, "The Light of the World Is Jesus," lyrics by Philip P. Bliss, public domain.

Chapter 13

". . . *therefore* this thing has come upon you"
(Jeremiah 40:3b).

The Lord spoke over and over to Jeremiah, the prophet:

> Jeremiah 25:8 "*Therefore* thus says the
> LORD of hosts: 'Because you have not
> heard My words . . . I will send . . . Nebu-
> chadnezzar, the king of Babylon, My ser-
> vant, and will bring them against this land
> . . . and will utterly destroy them . . .'"

> Jeremiah 28:16 "*Therefore* thus says the
> LORD: 'Behold, I will cast you from the
> face of the earth . . . (Jeremiah speaking
> to Hananiah, the prophet, for making the
> people trust in a lie) because you have
> taught rebellion against the LORD.'"

> Jeremiah 14:15 "*Therefore* thus says the LORD concerning the prophets who prophesy in My name, whom I did not send . . . 'By sword and famine those prophets shall be consumed!'"

> Jeremiah 7:16 "*Therefore* do not pray for this people . . . for I will not hear you."

God gave warning after warning for His people to repent (Jeremiah 7:3–4). God has given America many words of warning—repent, repent. America pauses for only a moment, then goes back to her sinful ways.

God finally got fed up with Israel and told Jeremiah not to even pray for them because He would not hear. Will God turn His ear away from America? Do we have one last chance? Will we STOP and LISTEN?

Will we pray and turn our hearts to Him before it is too late?

Chapter 14

"*Therefore* I hope in Him!" (Lamentations 3:24b).

―――――――――――

Why do I hope in Him? "Through the LORD's mercies we are not consumed, because His compassions fail not. They are new every morning; great is Your faithfulness. 'The Lord is my portion . . .'" (Lamentations 3:22–24a).

When I got up this morning, His compassions were new!

When our little baby, Philip, died—God was faithful!

When Adrian slipped into heaven—God was faithful!

When our little great-granddaughter, Poppy Joy, took her flight home—God was faithful!

As I live without my husband day by day, God is faithful!

I love to do word studies as I read my Bible. After Adrian died, I looked for verses about *help* and *hope*. What

47

an encouragement this was to me. Yes, He promised to give me *help* for today and *hope* for my tomorrows. I highly recommend this to you, especially if you're going through a difficult time in your life.

In a message from Lamentations the third chapter entitled, "Choosing Your Perspective," Adrian spoke these pertinent words: "What an incredible thing for us to learn that no matter where we are, how lonely the night, how dark the road, how big the problem, Jesus Christ is always there."

As you find and read these promises, *claim* them as your very own. You will see them come true in your own life and circumstances. This modern generation has tried to change the true meaning of hope. I was waiting to get a haircut recently and was flipping through a magazine. An ad for a facial cream "jumped off of the page" at me. It was entitled "Renewed Hope in a Jar." Then followed their philosophy: "When you renew with hope, wishes come true." What a distortion of true hope that comes from God. Hope in the Bible does not mean, "I *think* so!" Adrian said, "Hope is rock-ribbed assurance based on the Word of God enjoined with anticipation." So *why* should I hope in that One Who is called the Word of God? The answer is given in Lamentations 3:22–24. Jeremiah, the prophet, said:

"Through the LORD's mercies we
are not consumed,
Because His compassions fail not.
They are new every morning;
Great is Your faithfulness.
'The LORD is my portion,' says my soul.
Therefore I hope in Him!"

One of the greatest hymns ever written is "Great Is Thy Faithfulness." My daughter, Gayle, had this hymn sung by the congregation at her wedding.

Great is thy faithfulness!
Great is thy faithfulness!
Morning by morning new mercies I see;
All I have needed thy hand hath provided;
Great is thy faithfulness,
Lord, unto me![4]

"Now may the God of hope fill you with all joy and peace in believing, that you may abound in hope by the power of the Holy Spirit" (Romans 15:13).

---

[4] Hymn, "Great Is Thy Faithfulness," lyrics by Thomas Chisholm. Public domain.

Chapter 15

> "*Therefore* do not worry, saying, 'What shall we
> eat' or 'What shall we drink?' or 'What shall we wear?' . . .
> But seek first the kingdom of God
> and His righteousness . . ." (Matthew 6:31, 33a).

Christians in the United States are caught up in eating, drinking, and buying the latest fashions. Much of the world is at war and unrest is all around. When will we wake up? Jesus told us not to worry about all these outward things but to seek *His* kingdom first. He was not saying that we didn't need to eat, drink, and be properly clothed, but that this should not be our focus.

What does it mean to seek His kingdom? I believe, first of all, that at the beginning of each day we should study His Word and seek Him through prayer—express our love to Him, not to seek to know *about* Him, but beyond that to know Him!!

This passage of scripture goes on to say that we should seek His righteousness.

We should seek to live a holy life—not a self-righteous, but a truly righteous life. This will be a life pleasing to Him!

Then we should intercede for others—our family, friends, and acquaintances who have spiritual, emotional, and physical needs. Ask the Lord to show how we can genuinely love and minister to their needs. And yes, we should pray for our enemies. As I say this, I'm convicted that I haven't prayed for the Al-Qaeda terrorists around the world. Not that I should wish them "God speed," but that I should pray for their salvation.

We should gather with other Christians and agree together in prayer for our needs but also for the needs of our fellow Christians who are being persecuted and dying for their faith. We should pray for and share with those with whom we come in contact daily to remember how much Jesus loves them. Do some kind deed for that neighbor, the bank teller, the check-out lady at the drug or grocery store. Ask God to give you courage and boldness and love! Do it today! I will! Will you?

Chapter 16

"Therefore whoever confesses Me before men, him I
will also confess
before My Father who is in heaven" (Matthew 10:32).

———————————

Are you ashamed of Jesus? Do you try to hide that
you know Him? Then I wonder if you really know
Him. Jesus said that if we are not willing to confess Him
before men, He won't confess us before His Father. Is
there really such a thing as a "secret" believer or is this
an oxymoron?

Most of my everyday contacts are very brief.
There is no time to share *the plan of salvation*. The Lord
gave me a simple but profound greeting in these brief
encounters. I have said to many people, "Just remember
all day long how much Jesus loves you!" I've never
had a negative comment. One man at the curb check-
in at the airport reached out and hugged me. Only two
people have given no response. On some occasions, I
leave a gospel tract also. There are simple, unique ways

to "confess Jesus before men." Ask God to show you something to say, or borrow my idea, if it fits your style!

In Iraq, the terrorist group ISIS has told Christians that they must leave their homes, deny their faith in Christ, or be put to death. Many have stood strong and have been put to death for their faith. We in the United States have never really experienced persecution for our faith. Will we now be called upon to die for Jesus? Will many deny Him? May we be willing to confess Him openly even if it means that we must give our lives for Him!

Chapter 17

"Therefore I say to you, do not worry about your life . . ."
(Luke 12:22).

J esus admonished His disciples to "consider the lilies" in Luke 12:27. In Memphis, Tennessee, where I live, spring has just begun. Yesterday I took my friend Elizabeth to see the parade of white cherry blossom trees that line the drive in Audubon Park. They were at their peak and were glorious in their splendor. If God can clothe these trees with such majesty, why should I worry about how He might take care of me?

I don't go to Adrian's grave frequently. I know that he is not there but is with his Lord. However, I love to go there on Easter, for I am reminded that because Jesus was raised from the dead, there will be a day when He will come again, we will be caught up together to meet Him in the air, and we shall forever be with the Lord. I love to think of that day when the bodies of our loved ones who have gone on before will be raised incorruptible, and we shall all be changed.

The body of our little baby, Philip, is there also. At the rapture, he will also be raised. Hallelujah! We shall all be changed! We will be made like Jesus. I'm longing for that day. But until that day I will keep on trusting in Him to take care of me, and I will be looking for His return.

I just returned from south Florida where I visited with my sister Doris. She is a woman of faith and prayer, who is content with the little that she has and is not worried about tomorrow. Doris has a rare form of leukemia, and only God knows how many days she has before she graduates to glory! She talked about her *celebration service*, for that is what she wants it to be. It was wonderful to sit and talk about seeing Jesus face-to-face. We also reflected on good days gone by. We remembered loved ones who have already passed to the other side. I will miss my sweet sister. For many years now she has been my greatest prayer partner. However, I believe that when she is in heaven, I will still be able to count on her continued prayers. This one thing I know for sure—Jesus ever lives to make intercession for me in heaven. The Bible tells me so! (Hebrews 7:25).

Chapter 18

"*Therefore*, having been justified by faith, we have peace with God
through our Lord Jesus Christ" (Romans 5:1).

The world longs for peace—the absence of war, the opportunity to live quietly and enjoy the nice things of life. There is a modern song that goes this way: "I'd like to teach the world to sing, in perfect harmony . . . for peace throughout the land." It began as a Coca-Cola commercial back in 1971. It's a nice concept, but outward peace will never come until we first have peace with God.

Some say that there are many roads that lead to God and that Jesus is just one of these ways. But Jesus said, "I am the way . . . no one comes to the Father except through Me" (John 14:6). Indeed, Jesus is God Who came in the flesh. The angels heralded His coming saying, "And on earth peace, goodwill toward men!" (Luke 2:14). Jesus said before He went back to His Father, "My peace I give to you; not as the world gives do I give to you. Let not your heart be troubled, neither let it be afraid" (John 14:27).

Jesus can use us as ambassadors of peace. Second Corinthians 5:20 says, "Now then, we are ambassadors for Christ, as though God were pleading through us: we implore you on Christ's behalf, be reconciled to God." True peace works from the inside out. Ephesians 2:14 tells us that, "He Himself is our peace." We must invite Jesus, the Prince of Peace, to rule in our hearts. Then God can use us to help bring peace on earth.

Chapter 19

"*Therefore* we were buried with Him through baptism into death, that just as Christ was raised from the dead by the glory of the Father, even so we also should walk in newness of life" (Romans 6:4).

Baptism is a *living picture* of death, burial, and resurrection. First, it pictures the death, burial, and resurrection of Jesus. But don't stop there. It shows to the world my identification *with* Him. I died *with* Him—died to my *Old Sinful Self.* Then OSS was buried *with* Him. Second comes the picture of the resurrection. But it is not *Old Sinful Self* that is raised, but a brand-new life—raised to walk in newness of life! Yes, baptism is a picture to the whole world that because of Jesus I am a brand-new person.

In 1990, right after the fall of communism in Romania, about 170 people from our church took a mission trip to that country. The group was divided, and we were invited to work with members of different local churches. Adrian preached the gospel in large auditoriums in three major cities in Romania, including Bucharest.

Adrian and I were asked to work with Joseph 'Tson and his wife, Elizabeth, in the Second Baptist Church in Oradea, Romania. On Sunday, they were having a baptismal service. I had never experienced anything quite like it. Each person could make his or her baptismal garment. Some of the women made a beautiful dress similar to a bridal gown. What a preparation there had been! Each person had written out their testimony of how Christ had saved them. Some of these were presented publicly. Elizabeth translated for me. What a joy it was to celebrate with these new believers who lived half a world away from where I lived in Memphis, Tennessee.

I wanted to bring home the feeling I felt that day. Their baptism was such a joyous celebration! It was impossible to copy that experience. However, I decided that I would try to do what I could in my New Members' Class to impress upon the children how special baptism is and what it represented. I used pictures and diagrams of the Old Sinful Self as being dead and buried, never to rise again, but a brand-new life being raised. We should now live a resurrection life, depending on our risen Savior to live that life in and through us. As Major Ian Thomas loved to say,

I can't. He never said I could.
He can. He always said He would!

Chapter 20

"I beseech you *therefore* . . . that you present your bodies a living sacrifice . . ." (Romans 12:1).

When I was a teenager I memorized Romans 12:1. More than that, I told the Lord that I wanted to present my body to Him as a living sacrifice. I was challenged in my youth group at church to sign a pledge saying that I would never drink alcohol. I determined then that I would not take any harmful substance like tobacco or beverage alcohol into my body. I have kept that vow and I believe that God has blessed me because of this promise that I made.

When I was in my early forties, I adopted a lifestyle of healthier eating. Because I recognized that my body was the temple of the Holy Spirit, I wanted to glorify God in my body as well as in my spirit (1 Corinthians 6:19–20). I began to eat natural foods and cut down on desserts and high fatty foods.

In my thirties, I was tired all of the time. I am now in my early eighties, and I am reaping good health. In my mind I think I am fifty-five years old. I am still able to travel, drive my car, and live alone. I believe that a healthy lifestyle has contributed to this.

Trusting God in my spirit and thinking thoughts filled with faith are a big part of this blessing also. Not that I never get sick, but it is less frequent than it used to be when I was younger. I am so grateful to God for showing me a healthier lifestyle. God has blessed my life, and you too can be blessed by following God's guidelines for healthier eating.

Chapter 21

"*Therefore*, if anyone is in Christ, he is a new creation . . ."
(2 Corinthians 5:17).

"Something's happened to Adrian!" Those were the words of our ninth-grade teacher, Mrs. Gillum. I had not previously known of my boyfriend's reputation as a fighter—one who skipped school, cheated, and told lies.

I only knew him as the cute boy who had dropped love notes by my desk in the sixth grade. Incidentally, I still have those love notes. They must have made an impression because I *did* become Mrs. Adrian Rogers. Mrs. McCauley, our junior high school principal, sat in the congregation on our wedding day. She was the one who had called my mother when I was in the sixth grade to tell her that I liked the *worst* boy in school. You see, I was known as a *good* girl.

Indeed, something *had* happened to Adrian. At a revival meeting at the Northwood Baptist Church (just a block from where Adrian lived), he had stepped out during the invitation to receive Christ as his Lord and Savior, right behind his daddy.

After that, we began to sit together in church. I lived just a block from the church, across the street from our school and just two blocks from Adrian's house. We became very active in the youth group. Adrian and I attended church together every Sunday morning and night and every Wednesday night for prayer meeting. He walked me home from school and from church. By the time we were old enough to date, we already thought that we were in love.

When Adrian was sixteen and I was fifteen, we went with our pastor and a group from the church to the Ridgecrest Baptist Assembly in Ridgecrest, North Carolina.

I was standing by his side the evening he stepped out to go forward during the invitation to publicly declare that he felt that God was calling him to preach the gospel. There was no one in the whole world any happier than I. However, we were too young to declare our love for one another, but deep in my heart I knew that one day I would be Mrs. Adrian Rogers, pastor's wife.

Neither of us dreamed that one day he would become the pastor of the historic Bellevue Baptist Church in Memphis, Tennessee, and that God would use this man to help win The Battle for the Bible that would bring Southern Baptists back to their historic roots as people who believed in the inerrancy of the scriptures.

Yes, something *had* happened to Adrian. He had become a new creation. He was a pastor for fifty-four years before he graduated to glory at age seventy-four. Our missionary son, David, helped choose the scripture we placed on his grave marker—2 Corinthians 5:17 that says, "Therefore, if anyone is in Christ, he is a new creation; old things have passed away; behold, all things have become new."

Chapter 22

"Therefore be imitators of God . . . And walk in love . . ."
(Ephesians 5:1).

———————————

This is a song I sang in my youth group as a teenager:

> My desire, to be like Jesus
> My desire, to be like Him.
> His Spirit fill me
> His love o'erwhelm me;
> In deed and word
> to be like Him.

The thought behind these words has been the prayer of my heart for many years. When I sang this song as a young person, I did not fully comprehend what it meant—what heartaches I would experience along with many joys. God used each heartache to cast me upon Him and to make me more like Jesus.

God invited me to lay down my hurts and burdens at His feet and to be healed. No, He would not allow me to harbor bitterness. He knew that it would poison my soul.

In exchange for my surrender, He has fashioned me more into His image. Oh, He's not finished with me yet. But one day when I stand in His presence, the work will be complete. I will be just like Him! ". . . we know that when He is revealed, we shall be like Him, for we shall see Him as He is" (1 John 3:2).

So lay your burdens down. He is waiting on you—now!

Chapter 23

"*Therefore*, just as the church is subject to Christ, so
let the wives be to their own husbands in everything"
(Ephesians 5:24).

So many in this generation of women despise these
words. They do not want to be in submission to any
man. But we notice a *therefore*, so let's examine what it is
there for. Notice two little phrases—*just as* and *so let*. In
other words, in the same way that the church is subject to
Christ, may wives be to their own husbands.

So how is the church subject to Christ? The
church is the *bride* of Christ. He loved her, gave Himself
for her. If we are redeemed, we are part of His bride.
In return the church should willingly be in submission
to Christ, desiring to only do His will. He is a loving
Bridegroom, only looking for the very best for His bride.

He desires a pure bride—spotless, dressed in white.
In this life, He is purifying His bride, so she will not be
ashamed when one day she sees her Beloved face-to-face.

The relationship of husband and wife is supposed to be a picture to the world of Christ and *His* bride, the church. The wife, therefore, should lovingly submit to her husband. However, this relationship is not to be one sided. Verses 25–28 follow:

> Husbands, love your wives, just as Christ also loved the church and gave Himself for her, that He might sanctify and cleanse her with the washing of water by the word, that He might present her to Himself a glorious church, not having spot or wrinkle or any such thing, but that she should be holy and without blemish. So husbands ought to love their own bodies; he who loves his wife loves himself.

Who wouldn't want to be in submission to a bridegroom like that? But unfortunately, both the man and the woman are sinful and fall short of this beautiful picture and goal. We should continually endeavor to meet this goal, asking for the help of our heavenly Bridegroom. What a responsibility—to show the world the love of Jesus. "Oh, Lord Jesus, give us as women Your grace that we might be a beautiful, pure bride. And give Your grace to the men to love their wives as Christ loved the church."

Therefore—

just as

so let

Chapter 24

"*Therefore*, take up the whole armor of God . . ."
(Ephesians 6:13).

I was looking for some furniture for my new house. In a store that belonged to a friend, I saw something that caught my eye—a full-sized suit of armor. It was the neatest thing! The price was $150. I wanted to buy it, but what would I do with it?

The Lord gave me a wonderful idea. I could use it in my Children's New Members' Class to help teach the children about the armor of God as found in Ephesians 6:11–20. My friend sold it to me for fifty dollars and for many years I used it as an object lesson in my class. Only heaven will tell the impression this armored soldier made on the boys and girls. But I know the impact it made on my life.

The Belt of Truth

Let's think about the pieces of armor and what they represent. First, we should put on *the belt of truth*, which is so foundational in our Christian lives. King David declared in Psalm 51:6, "Behold, You desire truth in the inward parts." Yes, God Himself puts a premium on truth. You can't fake it. It comes from the inner being.

My husband valued truth—inner truth based on the truth of God's holy Word. He spent his life declaring God's truth. I too value truth. My father was also a man of integrity and greatly influenced my life. Yes, I will live and die for truth. My source of this truth is Jesus Who said, "I am the way, the *truth* and the life . . ."(John 14:6).

The Breastplate of Righteousness

Second, we should put on the *breastplate of righteousness*. The Bible tells us, "There is none righteous, no not one" (Romans 3:10). Romans 3:23 says, "All have sinned and fall short of the glory of God." Jesus took my sin upon Him when He died on the cross. He actually became sin for us. "For He made Him who knew no sin to be sin for us, that we might become the righteousness of God in Him" (2 Corinthians 5:21). Praise the Lord, I know I am righteous because Jesus is my righteousness. Now who do you think wants to lead you in your spiritual walk? Yes, it is Jesus! Psalm 23:3 (KJV) tells us that, ". . . he leadeth me in the paths of righteousness for his name's sake."

I love Psalm 71. It speaks many times of God's righteousness.

"Deliver me in Your righteousness . . ." v. 2
"My mouth shall tell of Your righteousness . . ." v.15
"I will make mention of Your righteousness . . ." v.16
"Also Your righteousness, O God, is very high . . ." v.19
"My tongue also shall talk of Your righteousness . . ." v. 24

The Shoes of the Gospel of Peace

Third, put on your shoes—"and having shod your feet with the preparation of the gospel of peace" (Ephesians 6:15). The whole world is engulfed in war. Unbelievable atrocities are being committed in the name of Allah. Christians are being beheaded, children are being killed, and women and girls are being forced into sex slavery.

In our own country, racial hatred is being stirred up. It is only the gospel—the Good News of Jesus' death, burial, and resurrection—that can bring lasting peace.

The Shield of Faith

"Above all, taking the shield of faith with which you will be able to quench all the fiery darts of the wicked one."

Yes, Satan is out to get you. He's hiding behind every bush and tree, ready to sabotage your every effort to live godly. Fourth, don't forget to take your shield— the shield of faith. Faith in yourself, faith in the church, your pastor, your Christian friends, or your family? No! At some point, these all will disappoint you. It is faith in the Son of God! Someone has put the meaning of faith in an acrostic—

F orsaking
A ll
I
T rust
H im

It is not a *head* faith that I need, but a *heart* faith. I love Psalm 56:3–4:

"Whenever I am afraid,
I will trust in You.
In God (I will praise His word),
In God I have put my trust;
I will not fear.
What can flesh do to me?"

The Helmet of Salvation

"And take the helmet of salvation . . ." (Ephesians 6:17a).

Fifth, salvation here is speaking about a continual deliverance from sin, not about being born again, which is a once in a lifetime experience. I'm sure that you are familiar with the saying, "You can't keep the birds from flying over your head, but you can keep them from making a nest in your hair." To make this possible, you must cover your head. The mind resides in the brain, which is in the head. All thoughts, good and evil, originate in the mind, so you must guard your mind.

We all need *daily deliverance* from sin after our initial experience of being born again. We must be careful what we put into our minds. Did you sing this little song as a child?

Be careful little eyes what you see
For the Father up above

Is looking down with love
So be careful little eyes what you see.

Other verses continue:
Be careful little ears what you hear.
Be careful little feet where you go.

The Sword of the Spirit

". . . and the sword of the Spirit, which is the word of God" (Ephesians 6:17b).

Another song we sang as children was:

The B-I-B-L-E
Yes, that's the book for me.
I stand alone on
The Word of God
The B-I-B-L-E

I have loved the Word of God since I was a child. To help me learn reverence for the Bible, I was taught to never put anything else on top of it and to treat it special.

Of course, as I grew older I realized that it is not the outward cover and pages that were so special—but the message it contained. I learned that "For the word of God is living and powerful, and sharper than any two-

75

edged sword, piercing even to the division of soul and spirit, and of joints and marrow, and is a discerner of the thoughts and intents of the heart" (Hebrews 4:12). Wow! Do you understand what that means? The Word of God is so powerful that it can tell the difference between the soul and the spirit. We can only see the body; however, we know that there is something else.

Sixth, without the Word of God, we would not know that with the soul we can know ourselves and other people, but with our spirit we can know God. Animals don't have a spirit. They cannot know God. Mankind is different. We can even discern between *what* we are thinking and *why* we are thinking. The Bible is such a marvelous book!

The longest chapter in the Bible is Psalm 119. It contains 176 verses—all about the Word of God. A few of these verses are as follows:

v. 50 ". . . For Your word has given me life."

v. 54 "Your statutes have been my songs . . ."

v. 86 "All Your commandments are faithful . . ."

v. 89 "Forever, O LORD, Your word is settled in heaven."

v. 105 "Your word is a lamp to my feet and a light to my path."

v. 129 "Your testimonies are wonderful . . ."

v. 140 "Your word is very pure; therefore Your servant loves it."

After I have put on the *armor of God*, then what? The battle of prayer begins. Satan will do all that he can to keep us off of our knees. "Praying always . . . in the Spirit . . . with all perseverance and supplication for all the saints . . . that I may open my mouth boldly to make known the mystery of the gospel" (Ephesians 6:18–19).

What is this all about? That I might boldly share the Good News—the gospel—about Jesus! It is about the death, burial, and resurrection of Jesus. Praise His wonderful name!

"Lord, help me to put on Your spiritual armor each and every day, praying always to give me boldness to share Your gospel!"

Chapter 25

"Stand *therefore*, having girded your waist with truth . . ."
(Ephesians 6:14).

———————————

I lived for fifty-four years with a man of conviction, courage, and compassion. Because we had been in love since we were children, we married young—when we were in our second year of college. Toward the end of our freshman year in college, Adrian became the pastor of a small Baptist church just eighty miles from school.

We both majored in religion and took many courses together. I was sitting by him in class when he began to *stand for truth*. He sensed that the teacher did not always agree with that Book that he held in his hand. Adrian studied outside of the classroom on his own and determined that he believed in the inerrancy of the scriptures.

The teacher declared himself to be neo-orthodox. He was not out and out liberal, but he cast doubts on parts of the Bible. Today that school is extremely liberal, an endorser of the homosexual lifestyle and allows open dorms and alcoholic beverages on campus. This is far from what it was like when we were there, but that is where a liberal interpretation of the Bible leads. It is no longer associated with conservative biblical principles. How very sad!

Adrian went on to stand courageously but compassionately for the truth of God's Word. He became a mighty expositor of the Bible and one who was noted for his passionate plea to *Come to Jesus*. These words were etched over the entrance of Bellevue Baptist Church: "O send out thy light and thy truth" (Psalm 43:3a, KJV).

These words, which became known as his *no compromise statement*, were quoted in his presidential address at the Southern Baptist Convention in 1986:

> One man on the peace committee of the Southern Baptist Convention said, "Adrian, if you don't compromise, we'll never get together." I replied, "We don't have to get together. The Southern Baptist Convention doesn't have to survive. I don't have to be the pastor of Bellevue. I don't have to live, but I'm not going to compromise the Word of God."

The prophet Isaiah cried out to Israel, "No one calls for justice, nor any plead for truth. They trust in empty words and speak lies . . . for truth is fallen in the street . . ." (Isaiah 59:4, 14) My husband preached a sermon on this passage in Isaiah entitled, "Snake Eggs, Spiders' Webs, and Traffic Jams." He, like Isaiah, cried out for a return to truth.

I have seen Adrian be willing to risk everything to stand for truth. He would have been willing to *die* for truth. I am proud to identify myself with him. I too would be willing to die for truth. I'm not exactly sure what those in heaven know about the thoughts and actions of those of us who have been left here on this earth. But I'm convinced that whatever he knows, Adrian would be proud of his children, grandchildren, and now even his great-grandchildren, as coming behind him they boldly take their stand for truth.

The Bible verse that he claimed for his offspring was Psalm 112:2b. "The generation of the upright will be blessed." And here is a promise that I have claimed for them: "The righteous man walks in his integrity; his children are blessed after him" (Proverbs 20:7).

Chapter 26

"*Therefore* . . . work out your own salvation . . ."
(Philippians 2:12).

"Work *out* your own salvation . . ." not work *for* your salvation, as many have taught.

Can you work it out in your own strength? Indeed not! Philippians 2:13 states, "It is God who works in you both to will and to do His good pleasure." My husband used to say, "He won't do it without you, and you can't do it without Him." The gospel songwriter Mylon LeFevre wrote his first hymn when he was seventeen years old, and the message stated that, "Without Him I could do nothing."

There is another *therefore* in verse 9. "Therefore God has highly exalted Him . . ." Let us look to see what the *therefore* is there for. It follows that magnificent passage on the exaltation of Jesus and giving of the name above all names. The reason is:

He is Lord!
He is Lord!
He is risen from the dead
And He is Lord!
Every knee shall bow
Every tongue confess
That Jesus Christ is Lord!
—Author unknown

Oh, I've been to the *empty tomb* in Jerusalem. It is there I loved to sing these words. I love to bow my knee and confess that He is Lord to the glory of God the Father!

High and lifted up and
Given a name
A name that is above
Every name.
Therefore God has highly exalted Him!
Why was He exalted?
What is that name?
Who is that man?
Oh, His name is Jesus!
Every knee shall bow to Him
Every tongue confess that
Jesus Christ is Lord
To the glory of God the Father!

Yes, He was given a name
A name that is above every name!
Oh, how I love that name,
I'll praise His name forever.
JESUS
Matchless, glorious name.

Chapter 27

"Therefore . . . forgiving one another . . . even as Christ forgave you, so you also must do" (Colossians 3:12–13).

———————————

One of the first Bible verses I learned as a child was Ephesians 4:32: "And be ye kind . . ." Then I added, ". . . one to another," then ". . . tenderhearted, forgiving one another," and finally, "even as God for Christ's sake hath forgiven you" (KJV).

I have had a number of occasions in my life to heed this admonition. I have been deeply hurt, and I could have grown bitter and harbored my hurt. If I had, then it would have become bitterness, then hatred. It was a deliberate choice on my part to love instead of hate, to return good instead of evil. To forgive and overcome hurt is a choice, then a process. I had to deliberately choose to forgive, and then the process began.

The devil doesn't give up easily, so he brings up the hurt over and over again.

We must give that hurt over to God each time we remember, claiming God's power to forgive. Eventually, we will see that the hurt subsides and God's love and forgiveness reigns.

There is a powerful incentive given to us to forgive those who have wronged us. It is found in the last part of Ephesians 4:32: ". . . even as God for Christ's sake hath forgiven you." If our great God reached out to forgive us through the death of His Son, how can we do any less? We cannot do this on our own, but God will enable us.

Jesus taught us to pray, ". . . forgive us our debts, as we forgive our debtors" (Matthew 6:12). Then that significant word *if* delivers a powerful punch. "For *if* you forgive men their trespasses, your heavenly Father will also forgive you. But *if* you do not forgive men their trespasses, neither will your Father forgive your trespasses" (Matthew 6:14–15).

It is rather plain and simple. Do you need and desire God's forgiveness? Then you must be willing to forgive. If you choose to *not* forgive, Hebrews 12:15 warns us, "looking carefully lest anyone fall short of the grace of God; lest any root of bitterness springing up cause trouble, and by this many become defiled."

Bitterness can eat at your soul, then spill over on your family and friends. They can also become embittered by your bitterness. Some are even bitter against God.

One widow wrote me that she was bitter against God—blaming Him for "taking her husband," when she had prayed for his healing.

Trust Him with your hurts. He'll make sure that things are made right. God's Word says, "Vengeance is Mine, I will repay" (Romans 12:19). Don't steal what belongs to God.

Chapter 28

"*Therefore* . . . having boldness to enter the Holiest by the blood of Jesus . . ." (Hebrews 10:19).

When I was a young teenager, my mother was subtly drawn into a false cult—Christian Science. She was looking for a healing, and this cult talked of so many *good* things. I asked, "Mama, don't you believe in the blood of Jesus?" And she replied, "Oh yes! Yes, I do!" I turned in the book of their false teaching, *Science and Health with Key to the Scriptures*. I read to her these words: "The blood of Jesus was no more efficacious to cleanse from sin when he was hanging on the cross than when it was flowing through his veins."

This group had also taken any mention of the blood of Jesus out of their hymnal. Their founder, Mary Baker Eddy, stated that sin was a "figment of the mortal imagination,"[5] erasing in her mind any need for the forgiveness of sin.

Praise God that my mother eventually saw the evil of this religion of good thoughts and turned from it. Nevertheless, it robbed my mother of many years of service to her Lord, for she had been a wonderful teacher in an evangelical church before that time.

Before Jesus died on the cross and shed His blood, an enormous veil covered the entrance into the Holy of Holies. But at the moment of His death, the curtain was torn in two from the top to the bottom, indicating that God Himself had opened the way into His very presence.

> I've found the way through the blood
> Past the veil
> To the Holy of Holies with God.
> There by His power over sin I prevail
> As I walk in the path He has trod.
> There in the presence of Jesus I stand,
> Glorified Son, at the Father's right hand.
> There I can plead, I can claim, I can have
> All that He purchased for me.
>
> —Author unknown

---

[5] Mary Baker Eddy, *Science and Health with Key to the Scriptures*, (Massachusetts: The Christian Science Board of Directors, 1994).

How sad, however, that so often we do not take advantage of this high and holy privilege. We are too busy, too distracted, to pause and claim the power of the blood of Jesus to enter His presence. We need to have a set time each day when we think on these things. Just because the veil has been torn does not mean that we should rush into His presence without reverence. The highest price was paid for this privilege. We should take off the shoes of our busyness and enter His presence with a humble heart filled with gratitude and love.

We should also teach our children to be reverent when they come into His presence by prayer. We should give honor and blessing and glory to His name because Jesus is the name above all names.

Yes, come! Come boldly to the throne of God because of the blood—the sacred blood of Jesus! It is no wonder that the Lord's Supper is so precious to me— the cup symbolizes the crimson blood, shed for me, and the bread that shows His body, given for me.

> Oh! precious is the flow
> That makes me white as snow;
> No other fount I know,
> Nothing but the blood of Jesus![6]

---

[6] Hymn, "What Can Wash Away My Sin?" lyrics by Robert Lowry, public domain.

Why are we to come boldly to His throne of grace? Hebrews 4:16 tells the answer: "that we may obtain mercy, and find grace to help in time of need." Which one of us doesn't have a need? Oh, praise His name! In our time of need, we can find help, mercy, and grace. Won't you come to Jesus now?

Chapter 29

"You *therefore* beloved, since you know this beforehand, beware lest you also fall from your own steadfastness . . ." (2 Peter 3:17).

We are warned in 2 Peter 3:17 that we should beware lest we fall back from our steadfastness. We must be diligent. What is the secret to keep from *backsliding?*

It is revealed in verse 18: "But grow in grace and in the knowledge of our Lord Jesus Christ." Yes, the key is to *grow* and to *keep on growing.*

If we are to grow, we must spend time with our great God. Time to study His Word—to discover WHO HE IS and time to pray—talking to Him and fellowshipping with Him. This will enable us to know Him intimately. As in a marriage, if we want our honeymoon to never end, we must "feed that love from day to day and week to week from the best resources of our living," as our marriage ceremony exhorted. If we want our spiritual honeymoon with Jesus to never end, we must be constantly feeding that relationship and be growing in our love for Him.

Even when we were in our seventies, when I heard Adrian's car in the garage, I would run to the door and hug and kiss him. We always held hands when we went for a walk, and we played lots of huggy bear and smacky mouth, as he used to say.

Are we eager to get up early so we can run into the arms of our Savior and spend time with Him? Remember, He is our heavenly Bridegroom!

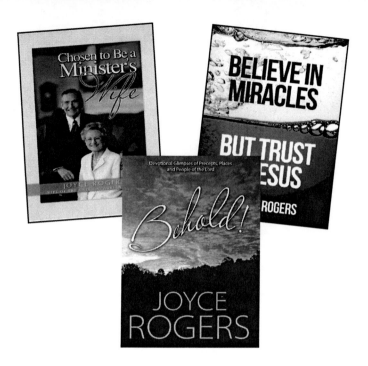

Order these additional titles by Joyce & Adrian Rogers:

CHOSEN TO BE A MINISTER'S WIFE

BEHOLD!

BELIEVE IN MIRACLES, BUT TRUST IN JESUS

innovopublishing.com

CPSIA information can be obtained at www.ICGtesting.com
Printed in the USA
LVOW08s1806170616

492988LV00001B/1/P